THE AMERICAN HORTICULTURAL SOCIETY
PRACTICAL GUIDES

OUTDOOR LIVING

THE AMERICAN HORTICULTURAL SOCIETY PRACTICAL GUIDES

OUTDOOR LIVING

STEVEN BRADLEY

A Dorling Kindersley Book

Dorling **DK** Kindersley

LONDON, NEW YORK, SYDNEY, DELHI, PARIS,
MUNICH and JOHANNESBURG

PROJECT EDITOR Simon Maughan
DESIGNER Janice English
SERIES EDITOR Annelise Evans
SERIES ART EDITOR Ursula Dawson
US EDITOR Mary Sutherland
MANAGING EDITOR Anna Kruger
MANAGING ART EDITOR Lee Griffiths
DTP DESIGNERS Louise Paddick, Louise Waller
PRODUCTION MANAGER Sarah Coltman

First American Edition, 2001
2 4 6 8 10 9 7 5 3 1
Published in the United States by
Dorling Kindersley Publishing, Inc., 95 Madison Avenue, New York, NY 10016

Dorling Kindersley Publishing, Inc. offers special discounts for bulk purchases for sales
promotions or premiums. Specific, large-quantity needs can be met with special editions,
including personalized covers, excerpts of existing guides, and corporate imprints.
For more information, contact Special Markets Department, Dorling Kindersley Publishing, Inc.,
95 Madison Avenue, New York, NY 10016 Fax: 800-600-9098

Library of Congress Cataloging-in-Publication Data

Bradley, Steven
Outdoor living / Steven Bradley
    p. cm. -- (AHS practical guides)
Includes index.
    ISBN 0-7894-7130-2 (alk. paper)
    1. Landscape gardening.
    I. Title. II. Series

SB473 .B66 2001
712'.6--dc21   00-056042

Reproduced by Colourscan, Singapore
Printed and bound by Star Standard Industries PTE Ltd, Singapore

see our complete
catalog at

www.dk.com

CONTENTS

THE YARD AS AN OUTDOOR ROOM

WHY CREATE AN OUTDOOR ROOM?

OVER RECENT YEARS, there has been an increasing preoccupation with spending more leisure time outdoors, particularly in the yard. This is a reaction to our changing lifestyle, both at work and at home. With more people working indoors than ever before, it is only natural that they spend as much leisure time as possible outside. On fine days, meals can be enjoyed outdoors, where they always seems to taste better and are eaten at a more relaxed pace.

CHANGING ATTITUDES

As the average dwelling becomes smaller, there is a tendency to treat the yard as an outdoor room, and it is possible to equip it with shelter, outdoor furniture, and outdoor lighting, all designed to extend the time spent in the yard.

For most families, the yard must provide an area for playing as well as relaxing. Safety is a major consideration, particularly where young children are concerned. Close to a busy street, the yard is an essential place for children to play where they are under the discreet observation of their parents.

SHELTERED SUMMER *Not all outdoor-based pastimes are active. For some, a beautiful garden spot offers a quiet place to sit and read or just to relax and watch nature at work. A permanent shelter, such as this summer house, can greatly enhance time spent outdoors.*

◀ ENTERTAINING OUTSIDE *Practical and atmospheric lights bring evening gatherings to life.*

PLANNING AN OUTDOOR ROOM

THE FIRST STAGE OF PLANNING is to decide what pastimes and activities you would like to use your yard for. If you have children, their needs will probably be your first and most major consideration. A property that has been divided into rooms often seems bigger and more alluring, because concealed areas retain a sense of seclusion and mystery. It also offers the opportunity to create spaces tailored to different uses, each with a distinct mood.

SEATING AND DINING AREAS

In an ideal yard, seating and dining areas are positioned in a sunny position as close to the house as possible. Such a site offers maximum convenience when preparing, cooking, and serving food, and it can be made into an extension of the house by adding a roof in the form of an awning, umbrella, or more permanent canopy.

If the sunny part of the yard is some distance away from the house, consider building the main seating area there. It may be a little less convenient, but a short walk is better than sitting in shade. On an exposed site, a screen may be essential to provide shelter from strong winds.

STORAGE SITES

Many of us do not have the luxury of a large yard, so a single area must be adapted to fit several uses. Storage is perhaps the biggest problem, but this is overcome easily with some imagination. The dead space beneath a raised floor of a shed, gazebo, or deck, for example, is usually forgotten, but with a hinged panel in the floor, tools, furniture, and toys can be placed out of sight and brought out when they are needed.

VERANDA WITH A VIEW
An area for relaxation can be many things; this veranda is the perfect place to sit and watch over life in the yard.

◄ SECLUDED SPACES
If size permits, divide the yard into a number of separate, but linked, areas – like the rooms of a house. Use trellises, plants, hedges, or fences as dividers, in place of walls.

▼ CONVERSATION PIT
Not all yards are built on a flat, level site, and this may appear to be a disadvantage at first. However, by combining raised beds with sunken paved areas, the lower level can be used to create an intimate area for conversation.

AREAS FOR CHILDREN

The most popular area for children of all ages is likely to be a open expanse of lawn as a general play area. Siting this away from the house, if possible, reduces noise

> A mature tree is the most obvious place for a play house or swing

and the risk of balls hitting house windows. If there is a mature tree in the garden, it would be the obvious place for a play house or swing. A tree used in this way also solves a common gardening problem, as the most difficult area to grow plants tends to be under the canopy of a large tree.

Eating and Entertaining

A COMMON FEATURE OF OUTDOOR ENTERTAINING tends to be the large number of people dining. Eating *alfresco* seems to be more of a social gathering than a meal indoors, and it often involves one or two barbecues, a large table or several smaller ones, lots of seats, a source of heat, and some well-positioned candles, lanterns, or electric lights (*see pp.20–23*).

The Choice of Furniture

There is a bewildering range of outdoor furniture on the market, in all styles, sizes, and qualities, and at all sorts of prices. If it is intended to be outdoors all year, rigid furniture is probably the best choice, but the real problem is which to choose. As well as choosing items in a style and color that will suit the yard or garden's design – be it modern or traditional – you will need to consider the practical aspects.

For durability and ease of maintenance, plastic furniture is very popular. It requires no painting or weatherproofing, although some less expensive kinds become brittle after several years of exposure to bright sunlight. Plastic furniture can look out of place in a very traditional setting, but its clean lines and bright colors are well suited to modern gardens or family yards.

Metal lawn furniture is less commonly seen, although there are some innovative contemporary steel seats and tables available, and some very good copies of traditional wrought- or cast-ironwork. This type of furniture is often very ornamental as well as functional, but iron will need maintenance, such as washing down and painting (*see p.76*), and it can be uncomfortable to sit on for long periods.

BREAKFAST
IN THE SUN
*In a small garden,
foldaway tables and
chairs are a wise
option, since they
take up little storage
space in winter, and
they are easy to move
about. Here, the
furniture has been
positioned to catch
the morning sun.*

A POPULAR CHOICE
*There is much to
recommend the use
of plastic furniture
in outdoor areas.
It is comfortable,
lightweight, easily
wiped clean, and
affordable. Many
colors are available,
so coordinating
furniture with the
yard's design will not
be difficult.*

On the other hand, there is aluminum, which has all of the good qualities of other types of metal furniture, but with the advantages of being light and easy to store.

Both plastic and metal furniture can be cold to sit on at times, and very hot during summer; the temperature of wood or

many people do prefer its natural feel. Choose from hardwood or treated softwood; both types can be stained or painted, if required, so that the furniture matches, or contrasts with, the rest of the yard, such as a neighboring trellis, fence, or planting display.

> ## The bright colors of plastic furniture suit modern lawns

wicker remains much more constant. The longevity of wood ultimately depends on the quality and how well it is maintained, especially in terms of weatherproofing (*see p.76*). Wooden furniture can be very heavy, but it is usually comfortable to sit on, and

SETTING THE MOOD

- When setting the table, make simplicity your goal and concentrate on comfort.
- Site a raised bed planted with fragrant herbs close to an eating area; the edge of the bed can be a good place to sit and talk.
- Decorate an entertaining area with flowers, for scent and color at different levels, from beds and pots to hanging baskets.
- Use lighting to create pools of light over a dining area. The soft and flattering flicker of candlelight creates a gentle ambience.

HEATING AND COOKING

Freestanding outdoor heaters have become increasingly popular because they extend the amount of time that can be spent outside on the patio or deck, especially early in the season and later in autumn. A range of patio heaters powered by bottled gas is available; they are designed to take the edge off the cool evening air by directing heat from head-height into a very local area. Braziers fueled by charcoal briquets perform a similar function.

Outdoor cooking seems to provide a focus for conversation. It is important, therefore, to choose a model that suits your cooking skills and available space, from the many charcoal- or gas-powered barbecues to one of the new generation of decorative garden stoves. These include compact, wood-fired terracotta ovens, which are shaped like

Outdoor cooking provides a focus for conversation

beehives and cook by radiant heat, and the kiln-fired, Mexican-style, chimney oven. Many barbecues and heaters are very versatile, since they can be moved or turned to overcome problems caused by changing wind direction, rain showers, or smoke.

HERBS AND FRAGRANT PLANTS

One of the advantages of cooking outdoors is that some of the natural food flavorings can be kept close at hand. Culinary herbs,

▲ MOVABLE MEALS
If different areas of your garden are in sun at different times of the day, a portable picnic bench may be a practical option. It is much easier to move around the yard than a set of individual tables and chairs.

▶ MODERN AND MOBILE
This stainless steel grill has a clean, modern design and is very practical. It is charcoal-fired and easily moved if smoke starts to blow in the wrong direction.

▼ CITRONELLA CANDLES
Insects can often be a problem outdoors. Lanterns or candles that burn insect-repelling oils, like citronella, will ward them off.

such as basil, bay, mint, parsley, rosemary, and thyme can all be grown close to the barbecue area and used fresh to flavor or garnish cold or cooked dishes. It is also useful to keep a potted *Aloe vera* plant nearby in summer; small sections of its fleshy leaves are very useful for treating minor burns caused during cooking, by smoothing the sap over the affected area.

Scented plants like jasmine and lavender are wonderful for providing a subtle fragrance on a warm evening when planted close to a seating area. Other plants make excellent insect repellents: tansy and pennyroyal are particularly useful for driving away those annoying visitors on a balmy summer's evening. If the area is to be used a lot at night, consider fragrant plants that flower only at night (*see box, p.21*).

The benefit of any of these plants, however, is lost if they are positioned too low, or too far away from, the sitting and dining area. The answer to this problem is to lift them up in raised beds or containers. A raised bed, up to about 30in (75cm) above ground level, will bring the plants much closer to people that are sitting down, and the edges of these beds make useful arm rests or improvised seats. Raising the plants also makes it easier to take care of them.

USEFUL PLANTS

Aloe vera Spiky succulent with thick, fleshy leaves filled with a soothing sap.
Lavender (*Lavandula angustifolia*) Low, gray-green shrub; scented, purple summer flowers.
Parsley (*Petroselinum crispum*) Clumping herb with distinctively flavored leaves.
Pennyroyal (*Mentha pulegium*) Spreading herb; aromatic foliage deters some insects.
Rosemary (*Rosmarinus officinalis*) Gray-green shrub; aromatic leaves and lilac-blue flowers.
Tansy (*Tanacetum vulgare*) Upright perennial; yellow summer flowers; deters some insects.
Thyme (*Thymus vulgaris*) Low, cushion-forming shrub with aromatic leaves and bright purple to white summer flowers.

A Space to Relax

R ELAXATION IS A FEELING of inner peace and tranquillity, and to bring this to your yard, you need to create a quiet corner or slightly secluded area. Here, you will be sheltered from the pressures of everyday life and surrounded by the timelessness of the natural world. Choose fragrant plants to scent the air and a small fountain to capture the relaxing sound of moving water.

FURNITURE FOR RELAXING

The lawn seating used for lounging and relaxing tends to be a great deal softer than furniture used in an eating area. Soft and natural materials, like cotton or canvas, are supported by a metal or wooden structure. The humble deck chair is a fine example: the seat molds around the occupant's body, and it is very comfortable. There is a wider choice of color and pattern available in soft furniture – choose a design that will not clash with the planting.

Rigid furniture can be made more enticing if it has removable cushions or paddings, but these will need to be stored away during wet weather or they will absorb water and start to rot. The main advantage of this type of covering is that it can give seating a dual function: the uncovered seating can be used for dining, while the covers or cushions can be added when it is needed for lounging.

Other types of seating are more self-contained, such as swing seats, which have their own framework and awning as well as fabric covers at the back and sides.

The color of furniture is an important element in lawn design

Perhaps the ultimate lounger is the hammock, either held within its own specially built frame or hung between two fixed points, such as sturdy posts or trees. These also have the advantage of being very light and extremely easy to store.

THE SIMPLE
THINGS IN LIFE
*A hammock is
probably the most
basic piece of yard
furniture you are
likely to come across,
but it cannot be
beaten when it comes
to relaxation. This is
the traditional sailor's
hammock, strung
between two trees;
many other styles
of hammock are
available.*

WATER AND WIND

The one element that is most commonly associated with a tranquil garden is water, and water features are always a good focal point in even the smallest yard. The soothing sound that water makes when it falls over stones or back into a pool can be very therapeutic, and this sound can vary greatly, depending on the type of feature, how and where it has been constructed, and the speed at which the water is running. Usually, the slower the water flow and the shorter the fall distance of the water, the softer and more relaxing is the sound of splashing.

Water features range from bubbling pools or wall-mounted fountains to streams and ponds, and – if the room is available – a swimming pool. More and more people are finding space to fit an outdoor spa, hot tub, or Jacuzzi as a watery source of relaxation. These installations can be partially raised out of a deck or patio, so major construction work is not an absolute necessity.

▲ TRANQUIL CORNER
This wall reflects both the sun's heat and the gentle sound of running water onto a secluded patio.

▼ POOLSIDE PATIO
The patio around this pool is a sun trap – ideal for sun loungers. The color of the paving is picked up by the cushions.

▶ ESSENTIAL FRAGRANCE
*Sprigs of common lavender
release an exquisite scent,
used in aromatherapy and
high-quality perfumes.*

▼ MUSIC OF THE WIND
*The random notes of a wind
chime cast a musical spell
on a garden.*

Many gardeners find the sound of the
breeze relaxing. Wind chimes come in
a range of materials, shapes, sizes,
and "tunes"; it should be borne in mind,
however, that some people find their gentle
tinkling very irritating after a while.

SPECIAL RETREATS

A relaxed atmosphere in which to sit
and read or simply to enjoy the garden
and its surroundings can be created under
a gazebo or arbor. Arbors are more
open structures, and they are particularly
good if you really do want to sit among
your plants. The entire structure can be
draped with climbers, such as roses or
honeysuckles, which have been trained
over the roof and sides to provide a
marvelous atmosphere of dappled shade
and natural fragrances. A well-chosen
mix of flowering plants will bloom from
spring well into autumn.

A more elaborate garden retreat with a
roof and solid or partial walls, such as a
gazebo or summer house, may have a more
utilitarian use in the colder months when
the weather can be uninviting. Then they
become storage areas for outdoor furniture
or portable barbecues (*see pp.28–29*).

An arbor can be draped
with climbers, such as
roses and jasmines

Children often try to create their own
retreat, and although much of their play
activity may involve expending a great
deal of sound and energy, especially when
several are playing together, there will also
be times when they prefer to play quietly.
Sandboxes and play pens are ideal for
young children, and they do like hideaways

or playhouses of their own. Here, scale is important; they enjoy places that are too small for adults to invade. Fold-away structures are increasingly popular, such as fabric tunnels and tents. These are perfect when the weather is changeable, because they provide somewhere sheltered to play. They are light and collapsible and can be put up by the children themselves.

A FRAGRANT LAWN

The most versatile area of the yard is the lawn, which may be used for games, relaxation, or just as an open area for all of the family to share. For such general use, a tough, hard-wearing turf that contains rye grasses is ideal. The lawn need not be restricted to grass; other ground-hugging plants, such as chamomile or thyme, may be used as an aromatic alternative. These plants release a sweet fragrance when crushed underfoot, but they are intolerant of heavy use. The non-flowering chamomile (*Chamaemelum nobile* 'Treneague') is suitable for lawns, as are the creeping thymes, such as *Thymus serpyllum* 'Annie Hall'.

PLANTS FOR AN ARBOR

Clematis 'Elsa Späth' Blue summer flowers.
Eccremocarpus scaber (Chilean glory flower) Brilliant, orange-red flowers in summer.
Humulus lupulus 'Aureus' (Golden hops) Beautiful, golden-green foliage all season.
Jasminum officinale (Common jasmine) White scented flowers from early summer to autumn.
Rosa 'Golden Showers' Fragrant, clear yellow flowers from summer to autumn.
Wisteria floribunda 'Alba' (Japanese wisteria) White flowers in spring or early summer.

▲ SOLAR POWER
Solar technology is a practical and safe alternative to outside electricity. This floating water fountain is powered entirely by the sun's energy.

◄ INSTANT CALM
A swinging bench with its own awning is a wonderful aid to relaxation. Its gentle movement induces a feeling of calmness and perhaps sleep.

TYPES OF COVER AND SHELTER

SHADE AND SHELTER ARE JUST AS IMPORTANT as open spaces in the garden. Whether they offer protection from the elements, such as hot summer sun, chilly breezes, or rain, or if they are used to create a secluded retreat away from prying eyes, there are a number of temporary or permanent structures that you can use in the garden. Thoughtfully placed, these structures can be attractive, and they will heighten your garden's design.

TYPES OF TEMPORARY COVER

There will be times when your enjoyment of the garden is impeded by rain or strong sun, equally unpleasant opposites. As a result, there is an increased tendency to use some type of cover in the garden to provide the necessary shelter.

For many gardens, umbrellas of various shapes, sizes, and colors are often the easiest option, but if a permanent structure is close by, such as a wall or fence, an awning is fairly easy to erect (*see pp.50–51*) and can be used to very good effect. The advantages of these types of temporary covers rest mainly with their flexibility;

the best ones take up very little storage space, and they can be folded up, opened, and erected easily and quickly.

PERMANENT SHELTER

Gazebos, pergolas, glass greenhouses, and arbors all offer shelter in one form or another. A greenhouse allows the yard or garden area to be enjoyed in cold or stormy weather, but you may need to attach shades

LIFE'S A BREEZE
This temporary awning, made from an old boat sail, not only shades the garden patio but also keeps the house cool by shading the windows.

◄ A DEFINED SPACE
This gazebo provides a secluded and sheltered spot in which to sit and ponder. Located opposite the house, it gives a refreshingly different perspective to the garden.

▼ SUN SCREEN
A garden umbrella is a convenient way to provide a small area of shade, especially if it can be tilted to follow the sun.

if you want to stay cool through the summer. Instead, you may prefer to move outside and sit under the shade of a flower-clad arbor or pergola, for example.

If your shelter has a roof, like that of a gazebo, it must be angled to allow the rainwater to run off. It also helps if the roof is

> Rain shelters must be able to let in maximum light

made of glass or thin canvas, which allows light to penetrate. This is particularly important on cloudy days or in the evening. Most important is to keep the sides of the structure as open to the light as possible.

SCREENS AND SECLUSION

Vertical screens are sometimes necessary to give shelter from wind, to act as a visual screen, or to create a feeling of seclusion and privacy from the neighbors. A wall or fence is one option, but a flowering hedge or a trellis planted with climbing plants, such as jasmines or roses, may be far more attractive. Living screens also make the best wind shelters; rather than forming a solid barrier to wind, which can cause turbulence, a hedge or trellis is slightly permeable, calming the wind as it passes through and leading to the creation of a calm, sheltered microclimate.

LIGHTING THE YARD

O UTDOOR LIGHTING HAS CHANGED THE WAY we look and enjoy the yard, and it is greatly under used. In effect, lights extend the time that we can spend outside. When used thoughtfully, lighting will add a new dimension of beauty to the area of the yard that it illuminates, highlighting the best features while the less favorable ones remain obscured in darkness. Practical lights also have their place outside, for reasons of safety and security.

LIGHTS WITH A FUNCTION

Outside lighting will often need to be functional, as a safety feature, to light paths, driveways, or steps, or as a security measure to deter nighttime intruders away from the house. Areas that are used for eating and relaxing at night are simply impractical without a source of illumination, but lighting in these areas goes beyond the purely functional; it can be extremely influential in producing just the right sort of ambience. When choosing a light, you need to consider not only the design of the feature itself but also the nature of the light that it casts.

Functional lighting that is subtle and decorative can be effective as well as easier on the eye. For example, a bright floodlight may seem like the perfect security device, but it blinds the home owner by casting deep shadows. Rather than deterring intruders, it provides them with someplace to hide. Most suppliers of garden lighting will offer practical advice.

▲ TRADITIONAL WALL LIGHT
Less harsh than a floodlight, this type of lighting is probably just as effective at deterring intruders at night.

◀ THE NIGHT LIFE
Illuminate the yard with several small and gentle lights to give a greater sense of ambience and a wider area of light.

◄ SUBTLE YET PRACTICAL
Discreet lights set into garden steps will illuminate a potential hazard, yet they won't dazzle or blind a passerby.

▼ HANGING LANTERNS
An overhead tree or structure can be used to hang an array of lanterns, but make sure there is no risk of setting the support on fire.

Path lights can be extremely discreet, especially if they are set into the path itself or into the risers of steps and stairs. It is important that this type of lighting is not too harsh; rather than acting as a guide, dazzling lights could cause you to stumble into an obstacle when moving through or

> Outdoor dining areas are simply impractical without lighting

into the illuminated area. Wall-mounted lights that are hidden but produce a soft beam of light directed toward the floor act as a guide without blinding the passerby.

DECORATIVE LIGHTING

Well-designed outside lighting brings a special beauty to the yard at night. It highlights the yard's positive features and draws the eye away from those areas we would rather remain unseen.

Many types of decorative lighting employ low-wattage lamps. If these types of lights are positioned in sufficient numbers, with the wires and fixtures skillfully hidden, the soft, scattered light they produce can be very effective and attractive.

NIGHT-SCENTED PLANTS

Cestrum nocturnum (Night-blooming jessamine) Pale flowers perfumed at night.
Gladiolus tristus Creamy yellow blossoms that are intensely fragrant at night.
Hesperis matronalis (Wild phlox) Delicious evening scent from white to purple flowers.
Matthiola longipetala subsp. ***bicornis*** (Night-scented stock) Pink, mauve, or purple flowers give a spicy scent at night only.
Mirabilis jalapa (Four o'clock flower) Fragrant flowers open in the evening and die by morning.
Nicotiana alata Long and tubular, green-yellow flowers with a strong fragrance open from early evening and into the night.
Oenothera biennis (Evening primrose) Fragrant yellow flowers open in the evening.

▶ LINE OF LAMPS
This multicolored series of lamps is pure decoration, and it livens up the dark shade of this wooden summer house.

▼ STRING OF BULBS
A string of small and white, bulb-shaped lights can be strung through a large tree or shrub for special celebrations. The smaller the lights, the more delicate the effect.

For areas devoted to seating and dining, the illumination of surrounding walls or screens can produce dramatic, atmospheric effects. Back-lighting uses low-intensity, wide-beamed lights positioned at ground level and directed upward to provide a wash of light over the wall's surface. Positioned behind pots or furniture, the lights are hidden, yet they create a stunning silhouette.

LIGHTING EFFECTS

• Direct ground-level lights at a blank wall or screen to create soft back-lighting.
• Suggest filtered sunlight or moonlight by pointing a wall- or tree-mounted light through a mature tree or down a wall.
• Use ground-level lights as spotlights to draw the eye to a particularly lovely plant or feature, or to create an intriguing or dramatic silhouette.
• Create pools or rivers of light by illuminating water features, such as fountains or waterfalls. Use special underwater lights only.
• Dot candles or oil lamps about to create an instantly intimate atmosphere.

> ### Upward-pointing beams create one of the most expressive lighting effects

Lighting from above is known as down-lighting, and it can be a way of imitating nature. Where light is directed through a tree or structure, such as a pergola, it emphasizes its form, suggests filtered sunlight or moonlight, and casts a soft shadow over the ground below. Down-lighting is ideal if the yard has a large, mature tree with a dense canopy.

The direction of light from ground level in an upward direction is used to highlight an attractive plant, to silhouette by throwing an outline into sharp relief, or to provide a focal glow in the yard. Up-lighting is one of the most expressive outdoor lighting effects, so long as it is used sparingly.

Subtle lights under the moving water of fountains or waterfalls can create magical effects, as do tiny lights strung around buildings or through trees or shrubs. Such lights are purely decorative, however, and they do very little to increase visibility.

CANDLES AND LAMPS

Although electric lights are often selected for their convenience, they are by no means the only choice. Oil-fueled lanterns or torches and candles of all sizes exploit the gentle and romantic ambience of a flickering flame. The range of styles of candles now available is vast.

The main drawback of outdoor lighting is that it serves to attract moths and other insects that roam around on summer evenings. To keep these creatures at bay, use lanterns or candles that burn insect-repelling ingredients, such as citronella oil.

In areas where people will be in close proximity to candle or torch lights, it is vital to consider safety. Open flames or hot surfaces must be placed out of reach, because they are dangerous to both children and adults. Even passing by quickly can cause some lanterns to flare up and become a hazard.

▶ CANDLE HOLDERS
There are a huge number of ways to display candles. Lanterns can be hung from hooks in brick or metalwork, or they can be contained in ceramic holders or glass tubes to offer protection from wind.

▼ WROUGHT-IRON TORCHES
These oil-fueled torches burn well outside, but open flames are a hazard. They are best avoided where children play.

CHILDREN'S PLAY AREAS

A CHILD'S IMAGINATION IS LIMITLESS, and almost anything has the potential to be turned into a toy or plaything. They will often try to create their own world, and most like to have structures that are too small for adults to invade or where adults are welcome only if they are invited. If you decide to include a play area in the yard for small children, with items like a sandbox or wading pool, make sure it is located close to the house, where children can be supervised.

HOW MUCH SPACE IS NEEDED?

For more active play, climbing frames, rope ladders, aerial walkways, swings, and slides are ideal, especially where several of these elements can be combined to provide a multi-activity area. Any of these structures can act as a focus for play, and draw the

children away from other, more fragile areas of a garden. Climbing frames will be much safer if they are built on a soft surface, such as bark chips, of at least 6in (15cm) thick.

Many of the ball games that children play require just a small amount of space. Games like tetherball involve a circular area of about 10–12ft (3–4m) in diameter. Basketball can be practiced in even less space, as long as there is a wall or fence on which to mount the basket. Both games can be played by groups of children in a relatively limited space and they can be set up without major work or expense.

GAMES ON THE LAWN

The traditional lawn should never be underestimated as a play surface. Not only does it have a cushioning effect when

▲ COVERED
SANDBOX
*This sandbox is easily
covered and stored
away if the lawn is
ever needed for a
different purpose.*

▶ RUSTIC LOOK
*This wooden climbing
frame looks like a
pergola; as a result,
it fits into the
traditional design
of this small garden.*

children fall down, but it can be marked and mown in such a way as to form specific play zones or courses.

Play structures, of course, do not need to be permanent fixtures. Temporary play structures come in a wide range of designs, such as collapsible or pop-up tunnels and fold-away play houses, which can accommodate up to several children at

> Even in a large garden, children tend to play in one small section only

a time and can be safely put up without adult help. These may provide valuable shelter in changeable weather.

There are also many toys, such as tennis or volleyball nets and basketball baskets, that pack away easily and take up little space when stored. If a lawn is used by both adults and children, the toys can be moved on and off the area as needed. They can also be moved around the lawn to prevent excessive wear on specific areas.

A BIG ADVENTURE
A large yard can afford to have a permanent play area for children. This one is built from smooth, rounded logs, which makes it safer.

For young children, the play activity may be more passive, and a shallow wading pool, a sandbox, or a small slide are more suitable. Small children, however, need constant – if discreet – supervision, so this type of play area must be as close to the house as possible. If you decide to install a permanent sandbox, remember that you could convert it in later years into a garden feature, such as a raised bed.

CHILD-FRIENDLY GARDENS

If the garden area is to be used also as a play area, the plant choice must be appropriate.

• Avoid plants that are poisonous or can cause blisters and skin inflammation.

• Avoid trees and shrubs with thorns or spines that may injure young children.

• Plants that attract wildlife, such as birds and butterflies, are a good choices. They will be a source of interest and education for children and adults alike.

SPACE FOR GAMES

FORTUNATELY, OUTDOOR PLAY is not the exclusive domain of children; families and friends of mixed age and sports abilities will often gather together to play or compete on a regular basis. This type of activity usually requires more space than areas dedicated to children's play, mainly because adults are bigger and the number of people involved is generally greater. If most games are to be played on grass, make sure the lawn will withstand the wear.

TYPES OF OUTDOOR ACTIVITIES

Besides gardening, active yard pursuits vary from games as gentle as croquet or giant chess to touch football or tennis matches. A lawn, although not essential, will be the preferred surface for many of these activities, simply because of its durability and versatility. Also, changes to field or net markings are very easy to carry out on grass when required.

Even games such as giant chess need little planning when played on a lawn; mow it from two directions and at two different heights to create a checkerboard effect on the grass before the game starts. It is even quite easy to create a maze on a lawn. Start by mapping out the required

SUITABLE LAWNS

• Use a grass type and mowing regime that is appropriate to the games you will play most.
• For ball games such as croquet, you will need a large, level area of fine grass.
• Lay down fine-quality turf for a putting green and cut with a reel mower.
• Active games, such as football or badminton, need a hard-wearing lawn. Opt for a turf that contains durable grass species, such as rye.

THE ULTIMATE OUTDOOR LUXURY
An outdoor swimming pool is on most people's wish list when it comes to leisure. As a form of exercise, swimming is hard to beat, and, on a hot summer's day, a pool provides a place to cool down and relax.

◀ GRASS MAZE
Rather than simply mowing a maze of temporary paths through long grass, the paths can be lined and covered with a thick bed of gravel to make a permanent feature.

▼ GAME ON GRAVEL
Gravel is more hard-wearing than grass and involves less maintenance. It is suitable for games such as lawn bowling.

pattern on the grass with sand or bamboo stakes as markers, and then mow the pathways through the long grass. The real beauty of making games areas in grass is that all it takes to reinstate the lawn is a sweep with the lawn mower.

LAWN SPORTS

For the more dedicated sports enthusiast, a 12–15ft (4–5m) area of closely mown grass can become the perfect practise green to hone golf-putting skills. No special equipment is needed, although a really fine finish to the turf does require a reel mower, which will cut grass very cleanly;

> Games like volleyball and softball can be played without access to a lawn

if it has a heavy roller, it will also create a striped pattern. To create the hole, a neat hollow can be made with a circular bulb planter. For those less serious about their golf, a few items of play equipment and garden furniture can be arranged as obstacles across the lawn to create an impromptu "putting green" course.

It is perfectly possible, however, to play a whole range of interesting outdoor games without having access to a lawn at all. Games like softball, touch football, and horseshoes can be played on a sand, gravel, or dirt surface, and tennis is often played on a range of surfaces other than grass. Volleyball can be played almost anywhere, and basketball just needs a firm surface where the ball can be bounced, such as a patio or driveway.

If you have the space, specialized areas can be set aside for specific games or activities. A permanent tennis court is likely to be the most common example of this, although a swimming pool is probably the ultimate dedicated facility at home.

SPACE FOR STORAGE

O NE OF THE MAIN DRAWBACKS of making full use of the yard is the amount of furniture, equipment, and toys that gradually accumulates, especially as different items are often needed at specific times of year. Storage areas do not have to be obtrusive or unattractive; they can be integrated into the design and even form part of a decorative outdoor feature. Look for an unused area in your yard; with a little imagination, it could make an ideal storage spot.

FINDING STORAGE SPACE

Storage is most important in small yards that have multiple uses. One way to ease the problem can be to select furniture and equipment that has several functions, such as seats that start out as dining chairs but can be adjusted and turned into lounger chairs. In yards with a shed or summer house, the solution to a storage problem is fairly obvious: these buildings are relatively waterproof and are often unused in winter, which makes them ideal storerooms.

It can be an interesting exercise to survey a yard and see how many areas of unused space can be found. A space such as the gap underneath a wooden staircase or raised deck – even a cavity of just 12in (30cm) in height and depth – can be sufficient room to store fold-away furniture, gardening tools, sun loungers, or play equipment. Decking that is laid in sections or panels can be adapted to include a removable or hinged panel, which will allow access to a storage cavity beneath the deck.

It is surprising to discover how many areas of dead space exist in a garden

Any space next to a barbecue could have a door or screen attached and can be used to store the charcoal, bottled gas, grills, and cooking utensils, which will keep them clean and neat. You could convert a wooden chair or bench into a storage seat by covering the bottom half with wooden panels and attaching a door or lid.

GAPS WITH USES
These gaps beneath a wooden seating area are home to quite a large amount of unused space. Sliding boxes could be inserted into the gaps, and simple doors fitted to make two weatherproof storage bins.

◄ CLOSED FOR WINTER
A summer house or gazebo, as well as being used for seclusion in warm weather, can double up as a storage space – especially for outdoor furniture – during the winter months.

▼ STORAGE BOX
Specially built storage boxes, whether made of metal or timber, can be strong enough to be used also as seats. Make a feature of a storage box by surrounding it with a trellis arbor covered with climbing plants.

Disguising Utility Areas

The most difficult things to store are large items in everyday use, which may be too cumbersome or heavy to maneuver from one position to another. For example, trash containers are generally unattractive, but they must be accessible. Some items, such as water and fuel tanks, cannot be stored; they are fixed in position. All of these things are better unseen, and the only option is disguise.

A recent development is the camouflaged trash container, which is covered in a printed design, usually of plants, so that it blends in with the garden. The most effective disguise is a living screen, such as a hedge or a trellis covered with climbing plants. Use plants with evergreen foliage where possible, so that the screen is effective at all times of the year.

PROJECTS FOR OUTDOOR LIVING

AREAS FOR EATING AND ENTERTAINING

CREATING AN AREA FOR ENTERTAINING in your yard can be as simple or as complex as your imagination allows. It may involve laying a patio, building a barbecue (*see below*), making garden furniture (*see pp.34–35*), painting a mural, or decorating a tabletop (*see pp.36–37*). Although some of these undertakings may seem daunting at first, they do not have to be. A good way to begin is to divide your plan into a number of manageable projects.

BUILDING A BARBECUE

Cooking outdoors, usually on a barbecue, has become an extremely popular outdoor activity. Portable metal barbecues are quite widely available, but they can be fairly flimsy and somewhat obtrusive in design, and they may need maintenance and storage over winter. It is amazingly easy to construct your own, more permanent, barbecue or grill using some basic building materials.

PERMANENT BARBECUES

- Permanent structures are the ideal option if barbecues are a regular summer activity.
- Brick or stone barbecues are safer to use. They are very stable, and the fire is well contained within three solid walls.
- Permanent barbecues can be made of brick or stone with a grill and grate inside.
- Choose brick or stones that blend with the style of your house, patio, and garden.
- Storage shelves can be built into the design.

THE GROUNDWORK
Unstable brick walls are dangerous, so always build on a solid foundation. Patio paving slabs make a good base; lay them on compacted hardcore and sand, topped with a layer of mortar. Check that the patio surface is level before building.

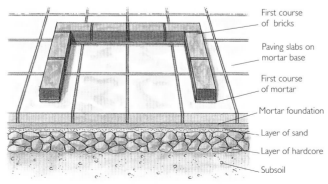

First course of bricks

Paving slabs on mortar base

First course of mortar

Mortar foundation

Layer of sand

Layer of hardcore

Subsoil

BUILT-IN BARBECUE *A solid brick barbecue is stable, safe, and long-lasting.*

YOU NEED:

- Approximately 130 fireproof bricks
- Mortar mixed from 2 parts soft sand to 2 parts sharp sand to 1 part cement (*see p.70*)
- 12 galvanized metal brackets
- Metal grill plate, 24in (60cm) × 15in (38cm)
- Metal ash tray, 24in (60cm) × 15in (38cm)
- Pencil
- Measuring tape
- Builder's set square
- Ruler
- Builder's trowel
- Cold chisel
- Mallet
- Level
- Pointing trowel
- Bucket handle tool
- Stiff-bristled brush

LAYING THE FIRST BRICKS

1 **Mark out the site** 24in (60cm) long and 15in (38cm) wide. The open side must face the front, and check the angles with a set square.

2 **Lay a bed of mortar** along the outside of the marker line. The mortar bed should be about 4in (10cm) wide and ¾in (2cm) thick.

3 **Lay the first course** of bricks onto the bed of mortar. Butter the end of each brick with mortar (*see inset*) before laying it. Press the bricks down gently.

BUILDING UP THE BARBECUE

1 **Halve several bricks** using a cold chisel and mallet. Mark the bricks first, and chisel all 4 sides for a clean break. Smooth the ends of the half bricks with the chisel.

2 **Position the second course** of bricks, using the half bricks to create a staggered bond, which creates a stronger structure. Regularly check that everything is in line using a level. Repeat this process for all the remaining courses.

INSERTING THE GRILL SUPPORTS

1 Make sure that the wall is vertical using the level. Gently knock any misplaced bricks into position, if needed.

2 Place 4 metal brackets between the sixth and seventh courses of bricks. These will support the ash tray.

3 Position more brackets between the eighth and ninth, then eleventh and twelfth, courses. The ends of the brackets should protrude by about 1in (2.5cm).

FINISHING OFF THE BARBECUE

1 Lay the final course of bricks with their flat surfaces facing up. With a pointing trowel and bucket handle tool, clean up the lines of mortar between the bricks (see inset). Both processes will help water run off the brickwork. Brush off excess mortar.

2 When the mortar is dry, after about 24 hours, slide the metal grill plate and ash tray into place so that they rest on the metal brackets. To vary the cooking temperature, place the cooking grill on either the top or middle brackets.

3 The finished barbecue stands about 3ft (1m) high. The ash tray and grill pieces can be removed easily for cleaning; they should be stored away when not in use.

ASSEMBLING A WOODEN CHAIR

Wood is a warm and comfortable material to work with, and it blends into the yard and garden well. Many types of wooden furniture are available in easy-to-assemble kit form, so you need not be an experienced carpenter to build them. These instructions are for an armchair with a single seat. All wooden furniture should be treated with a suitable preservative once every year (*see p.76*); a colored stain is used here to enhance the look of the wood.

YOU NEED

- 2 armrests
- 2 wooden dowels
- 2 side panels
- 4 screws
- 4 bolts with washers and nuts
- 4 screw bolts
- Seat section
- Backrest panel
- Wood preservative
- Hammer
- Screwdriver
- Adjustable wrench
- Medium sandpaper
- Paintbrush

BEFORE YOU START

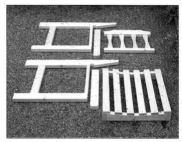

LAY OUT THE MATERIALS
Be sure that you have all the materials necessary by laying them all out on the floor. Compare what you have with the list in the instructions.

KIT ASSEMBLY

- Take time to read the instructions carefully.
- If any of the predrilled holes or joints are too tight, use a drill or sandpaper to increase their size slightly.
- Make sure all screws and bolts are hammered or screwed down tightly so that the heads are slightly below the surface of the wood and cannot cause injury or snag clothing.

ASSEMBLING THE KIT

1 **Gently hammer** a wooden dowel into the predrilled hole on the underside of an armrest. Use gentle force only, or you may damage the dowel – if the predrilled hole is not large enough, use a drill to make it slightly larger.

2 **Fit the armrest's dowel** into the predrilled hole on the top of one of the side panels. Swivel the armrest around, and push its back end into the rabbet on the back leg of the side panel. It should be a snug fit.

3 **Attach the armrest** to the side panel with 2 screws. The armrest is now centered over the top rail of the side panel. Fit the second side panel in the same way.

4 Attach seat section to one of the side panels by inserting 2 bolts through the predrilled holes. Fit washers and nuts to the bolts, and secure with an adjustable wrench.

5 Fit the second side panel to the seat section with the remaining bolts, nuts, and washers. Tighten all the bolts securely with the wrench.

6 Attach the backrest panel to both side panels with the screw bolts. Start with the bottom 2 predrilled holes, and only partly screw in the bolts. Rotate the back panel so the top 2 holes line up, then fit the last 2 screw bolts. Fully attach all 4 screw bolts, but be careful not to overtighten them.

7 Fully sandpaper all surfaces to avoid the risk of splinters. Double check that all joints are tight before you use the chair.

PAINTING AND PRESERVING

2 Allow the finished chair to dry for 24 hours before use. Apply a second coat of preservative, if necessary.

1 Treat the chair with a wood preservative (here, one with a blue stain). Do not overload the paintbrush, and follow the grain of the wood with your brush strokes (see inset).

MAKING A MOSAIC TABLETOP

Mosaic is not difficult, it requires only patience, a bold design for success, and a pair of eye protectors for safety. For the thrifty-minded, it is a wonderfully economic way to use up the odd, chipped, and broken tiles that shops are eager to dispose of. Keep the color range limited, otherwise small objects like this blue and white tabletop can look too busy and somewhat chaotic.

YOU NEED

- Circular wooden tabletop and metal base
- Navy blue, mid-blue, light blue, and white ceramic tiles
- Ceramic glue
- Strip of lead, the circumference and depth of the tabletop
- 20 × 1in (2.5cm) nails
- Gray tile grout
- Marker pen
- Mosaic tile nippers
- Eye protectors
- Spatula
- Scissors
- Hammer
- Small paint roller
- Sponge or damp cloth
- Soft cloth
- Polish

PREPARING THE MOSAIC

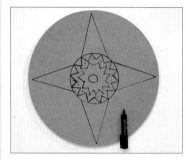

1 **Draw a simple** design outline, using a marker pen, on top of the circular tabletop. This compass design is composed of triangles and concentric circles.

2 **Cut the ceramic** tiles into small pieces using mosaic tile nippers. Cut rectangles for the border circles and irregular pieces for the central design. Wear eye protectors to shield against flying chips.

MATERIALS FOR MOSAICS

The small pieces of glass, tile, or stone used in mosaic are called tesserae. Glass and ceramic tiles are obtainable from special mosaic suppliers, either by the sheet in single colors or in mixed bags. Use mosaic nippers to break these tiles into even smaller pieces, if necessary. You may wish to experiment with other, more unusual tesserae materials for your mosaic, such as old or broken crockery, mirror fragments, pebbles, sea shells, and even flat-backed semiprecious gemstones. Make sure the tiles and other tesserae are all the same thickness and texture, or the finish will be uneven.

BROKEN MIRROR TILES

CERAMIC TILES

BROKEN CROCKERY

MOSAIC TILES

BUILDING UP THE MOSAIC

1 **Using a spatula,** apply glue to the central design. Place pieces of tile onto the glue, leaving a slight gap between each piece. Use the nippers to make smaller shapes, if needed.

2 **Build up** the surrounding area with more glue and the rectangular tile pieces to make a pattern of circles. When all the mosaic is in place, let it dry for 24 hours.

3 **Wrap a strip of lead** around the tabletop and cut it to fit, using scissors. Attach the lead strip by hammering in nails at 4in (10cm) intervals, and then two at each end.

4 **Apply gray tile grout** (mixed to a mud-pie consistency) over the mosaic with a small paint roller. Clean off the excess with a sponge or damp cloth and let it dry.

FINISHED TABLETOP
When dry, polish the surface of the mosaic with a soft cloth and attach the tabletop to the table base. This design was inspired by a seafarer's compass, a strong motif in a variety of cool, nautical blues. As a result, it would be the perfect perch for a croissant and coffee in the garden, or for a potted plant or two on the porch.

CREATING ATMOSPHERE

AREAS FOR RELAXATION ARE POSSIBLY the most rewarding schemes to create. Lighting and water are two of the most important elements in creating the appropriate ambience, and they can feature in a variety of installations. To begin, concentrate on items that will be the most useful, such as a well-placed outdoor light, and try not to be too ambitious by undertaking major projects that will take a long time to complete.

INSTALLING A WALL-MOUNTED LIGHT

Outdoor lighting may be essential for safety or security, and with a little thought, the same lights can be used to create a subtle ambience. Wall-mounted lights take up very little room and can be relatively unobtrusive. In many cases, electric wires need to be led across the yard to a light fixture, which is demonstrated in this project. The safest place to bury wire is alongside paving or under a lawn, where digging is unlikely. If you are forced to lay wiring through a frequently dug border, make sure the cable is laid at least 10in (25cm) deep and enclosed by a thick, brightly colored pipe.

ELECTRICAL WIRING
Most outdoor lights are powered by electricity, either directly or passed through a transformer to produce low-voltage current. They are best mounted on a permanent structure, such as a brick wall or stone post.

SAFETY FIRST
• All high voltage equipment must be installed by a qualified electrician, and the system must be protected by a ground fault circuit interrupter (*see p.74*).
• Run electric wires through a brightly colored conduit, so it can be easily seen if accidentally disturbed.
• Only use equipment that has been safety-approved for outdoor use.

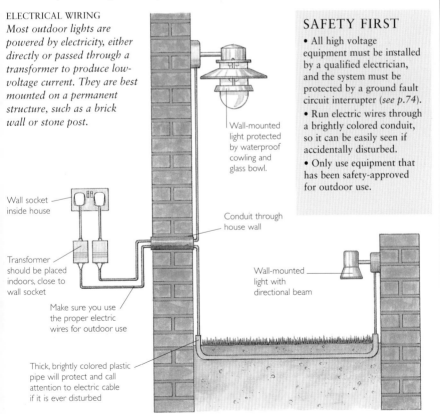

Wall-mounted light protected by waterproof cowling and glass bowl.

Wall socket inside house

Transformer should be placed indoors, close to wall socket

Make sure you use the proper electric wires for outdoor use

Conduit through house wall

Wall-mounted light with directional beam

Thick, brightly colored plastic pipe will protect and call attention to electric cable if it is ever disturbed

◀ NIGHT LIGHTS *Lighting set into and above these steps is for safety as well as decoration.*

YOU NEED

- Brightly colored hosepipe
- Outdoor electrical wire
- Wall-mounted light with light bulb
- Cable grips with nails
- 2 × 2½in (6cm) masonry screws with wall plugs
- 2 bolts
- Spade
- Brush
- Chalk or colored pencil
- Hammer
- Electric drill
- Screwdriver
- Adjustable wrench

LAYING CABLE ALONG A PATH

1 Dig a shallow trench along the edge of the path with a spade. The trench needs to be only slightly deeper than the paving stones, because you are unlikely to dig this close to the path again when working on the border.

2 Feed the outdoor wire through the hosepipe. This shields the wiring and makes it more visible if disturbed.

3 Lay the cable in the trench. If possible, push the cable just under the lip of the paving for added protection.

4 Cover up the cable with soil, or turf if the path butts up to a lawn. Remove any dirt on the path with a brush.

ATTACHING CABLE TO THE WALL

1 Clearly mark the exact position of the light on the wall with chalk or a colored pencil. Use the light itself as a template. Measure out the correct length of outdoor wire.

2 Attach the wire to the wall using cable grips. Where possible, run the wire along the line of a mortar joint to help disguise it. Make sure the wire remains taut.

CONNECTING THE WALL-MOUNTED LIGHT

1 **Mark the wall** to show where the drill holes are to be made. Use the back plate of the light fitting as a template. Remove the back plate and make the marks clearer, if necessary.

2 **Drill a hole** at each of the marked positions, slightly deeper than the length of the wall plugs. Insert a wall plug into each hole (*see inset*).

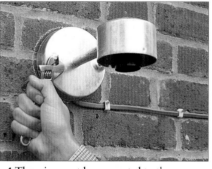

3 **Attach the back plate** of the light securely to the wall using a screwdriver and 2 masonry screws. It will be easier to use an electric drill if it has the appropriate attachment, rather than using a screwdriver.

4 **The wire must be connected** to the terminals in the front cover of the light fixture; then, bolt the front cover to the back plate with a wrench. It is always advisable to use the services of a qualified electrician.

5 **Insert a light bulb** into the fixture, then screw on the cowling and glass bowl. Check that the light and outdoor wires are both attached securely to the wall, and that all electrical connections have been approved by a qualified electrician.

6 **Condensation may collect** in the glass bowl, which may need emptying and cleaning occasionally.

MAKING A SOLAR-POWERED FOUNTAIN

Many people are reluctant to install a fountain in the garden because of the potentially hazardous electrical work involved. Solar-powered water pumps, however, require absolutely no involvement with electricity, and the risk of shock is negligible. This small fountain is safe to have around children, and instead of glass, a shatter-proof acrylic solar panel is used.

PUTTING IN A WATER RESERVOIR

1 **Mark out the area** where the reservoir will be recessed into the soil. A 5 gallon (20 liter) container for a reservoir will hold enough water to ensure the pump functions efficiently.

2 **Dig a hole** deep and wide enough to accommodate the reservoir. Remove any large or sharp stones from the sides or base of the hole, since they may damage the reservoir.

YOU NEED
- Reservoir tank
- Water pump approved for use with solar-powered systems
- Strong wire
- Brick
- Acrylic solar panel
- Fine wire mesh
- Plastic sheeting
- Large stone slab with predrilled hole
- Pebbles and stone chips
- Bamboo stake
- Spade
- Level
- Wire cutters
- Scissors

3 **Loosen the soil** in the bottom of the hole before lowering in the reservoir and seating it into position so that the top is level with the soil. This will allow the soil to settle evenly as the reservoir fills with water.

4 **See that the reservoir** is level once it is in the hole. Next, pack soil firmly around the sides of the reservoir. This will prevent its sides from buckling outward and possibly splitting once it is full of water.

INSTALLING THE WATER PUMP

1 **Attach the water pump** to a brick using strong wire. This will keep the pump stable, reducing vibration and possible damage.

2 **Fill the reservoir** about two-thirds full of water, then lower in the brick and pump. Allow any air trapped in the pump to escape.

3 **Connect the solar panel's** cable to the pump to check that everything works. Adjust the pump outlet so the top is just above the rim of the tank.

4 **Place a piece** of fine wire mesh so it covers the reservoir and 6in (15cm) of the surrounding soil. Cut a small hole in the mesh so the pump outlet can protrude through it.

5 **Cover the mesh** with plastic sheeting or pond liner. Cut a hole in the middle for the pump outlet, and make some small slits to allow water to drain back into the reservoir.

FINISHING OFF THE FOUNTAIN

1 **Place the stone slab,** fitting the pump outlet into the pre-drilled hole. Decorate with pebbles and chips.

2 **Move the solar panel** to a discreet position facing the sun; a series of solar panels will create more power.

COVER AND SHELTER

MAKING A COVERED OR SHELTERED AREA within a yard can be as simple or as complicated as you wish. The aim may be to construct a simple and removable canopy or awning, which can be put up when needed to give shelter from the sun during the hottest summer days. Permanent structures, such as gazebos, pergolas, or even small summer houses with glass doors and windows, can be put to practical use throughout the year. These outdoor buildings can be decorated with an imaginative selection of plants to soften the structure; use fast-growing annual climbers while perennial plants establish themselves.

ASSEMBLING A GAZEBO

A gazebo is a structure with a solid roof and partially open sides from which to enjoy the garden. Basic kits like this one can be bought from a fence or shed supplier. They are relatively easy to construct, but you must start with a firm, level foundation. Also check with your local authority before you assemble any large garden feature; building permits may be necessary for structures over about 8ft (2.5m) in height.

The wood in most kits is pressure-treated with wood preservative and predrilled with holes for the joints. These instructions are for an octagonal gazebo kit, 10ft (3m) tall and 8ft (2.5m) wide.

A hand screwdriver is acceptable for the job, but an electric drill with a screwdriver attachment is recommended for speed and ease. A sturdy stepladder is essential for work to be done above head height.

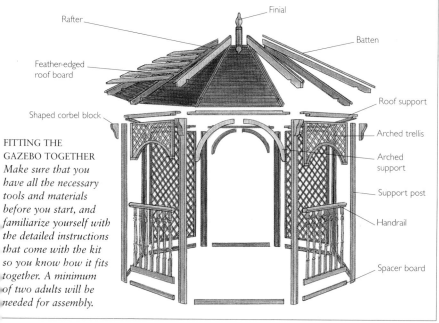

FITTING THE GAZEBO TOGETHER *Make sure that you have all the necessary tools and materials before you start, and familiarize yourself with the detailed instructions that come with the kit so you know how it fits together. A minimum of two adults will be needed for assembly.*

ELEGANT HIDEAWAY *This gazebo with fretwork panels is decorative as well as functional.*

YOU NEED

- 8 square posts
- 8 shaped corbel blocks
- 3in (7cm) screws
- 16 angled moldings
- 1½in (4cm) screws
- 1in (2.5cm) screws
- 16 metal angle brackets
- 8 spacer boardss
- 8 roof supports
- 1 finial
- 8 rafters
- 3½in (9cm) screws
- 8 battens
- 1½in (4cm) nails
- Precut feather-edged roof boards
- 2 trellis panels
- 2 arched trellis panels
- 2 handrail panels
- 8 arched supports
- Tape measure
- Pencil
- Screwdriver or drill with attachment
- Level
- Hammer

PREPARING THE SIDE FRAMES

1 **Mark the position** for a shaped corbel block 1¾in (4.5cm) from the top of each square post using a tape measure and pencil.

2 **Position a shaped** corbel block to the marked line. Attach it in place with 3in (7cm) screws. Repeat for the remaining 7 posts.

3 **Position an angled molding** along the length of one side of a square post. The steepest face of the molding should align with the front face of the post (the face with the corbel).

4 **Secure the molding** in place using 1½in (4cm) screws; put another on the opposite side of the post. Attach moldings to other posts in the same way to create 8 support posts.

5 **The finished support posts** have one shaped corbel block at the top of the front face, and angled moldings on either side. Check that all the joins are secure and safe.

6 **Attach metal** angle brackets to either end of a spacer board using 1in (2.5cm) screws. Fit the rest of the brackets to the remaining spacer boards.

7 **Fit the end** of a spacer board to the base of a support post. Use a 1in (2.5cm) screw to attach it to the molding. Make sure the bases and post are aligned.

8 **Measure and mark** the relative position of a roof support against a support post. This will ensure even positioning.

9 **Rest the roof support** on top of the shaped corbel block on the support post. Attach it securely in place with 3in (7cm) screws.

10 **Attach another** support post to the other ends of the spacer and roof support to create a frame. Make 3 more frames in the same way.

PUTTING THE SIDE FRAMES INTO POSITION

1 **Hold 2 side frames** upright, and fit a spacer board between them. With brackets and 1in (2.5cm) screws, first fit spacer to the base of the frames, then fit a roof support between their tops. The angle of the molding ensures that the frames are held at the correct angle.

2 **Add another** side frame to the gazebo as in step 1. The structure should now stand without any support.

3 **Attach the fourth** side frame to the gazebo as in step 1. Use a stable stepladder to reach the roof supports.

4 **Attach the remaining** roof supports and spacers to complete the octagon. Place a level across the top to check that the gazebo is level. Make sure that the structure stands solidly and safely, and retighten any joints as necessary.

MAKING THE ROOF

1 **Mark finial** 3in (7cm) down on each of its faces. Line up 2 rafters to the marks on opposite sides, attach to finial with screws.

2 **Lift the rafters** onto the roof support frame so they sit on 2 support posts. Secure the floating ends of the rafters to the roof support frame with 3½in (9cm) screws.

3 **Work around** the structure fitting the remaining rafters into place. For each rafter, fit the bottom first, then attach the top after lining it up to the mark on the finial.

4 **Position a batten** down the middle of one of the rafters. Fit it into place by hammering about 7 nails along its length. Work around the roof until all 8 battens are in place.

5 **Begin to nail down** the feather-edged roof boards. Work on one roof section at a time; start with the longest roof board at the bottom, which should overhang the edge slightly.

6 **Work toward** the finial, fitting each roof board securely between the battens so that they overlap one another by about ¾in (2cm). Continue until all the roof sections are fitted.

Finishing off the Gazebo

1 Fit a trellis panel into the rear left side frame with 3in (7cm) screws. Fit a second one into the rear right side frame.

2 Fit an arched trellis into the front left side frame with 3in (7cm) screws. Fit another into the front right frame.

3 Attach the handrail panels beneath each arched trellis with 3in (7cm) screws. Check that they are completely level.

4 Position an arched support in one top corner of the front side frame. Attach the arched piece to the support post and the roof support with 3in (7cm) screws.

5 Fasten a second arch to the front side frame to complete the archway. Use the remaining arches to install archways on the left, right, and rear side frames.

6 Remove spacer boards from front, left, right, and rear entrance ways once the gazebo is fully constructed.

PLANTING GUIDE

• Grow climbing plants in containers and train them through the trellis panels to clothe the structure.

• For summer shade, use large-leaved climbers such as *Vitis coignetiae*, which also colors well in autumn.

• For winter interest, plant evergreens with attractive foliage, such as ivy.

PUTTING UP AN AWNING

A simple awning can be an effective shade screen, and it is less formal and easier to erect than an elaborate structure, such as a pergola. An awning made from sail canvas, such as this one, brings a seaside atmosphere to the yard. An existing wall, a couple of trees, or a few heavy-duty posts can be used to give the required height, so very little construction work is needed.

YOU NEED

- 2 × 4in (10cm) expanding wall hook bolts
- Large canvas awning with reinforced a brass eyelet at each corner
- 2 × 12ft (4m) lengths of nylon cord
- 2 × 7ft (2.2m) plastic-coated or galvanized metal posts
- 4 sturdy tent pegs
- Chalk or colored pencil
- Tape measure
- Electric drill with masonry bit
- Wrench
- Mallet

INITIAL PREPARATION

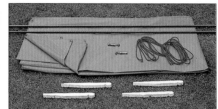

1 **Assemble all the materials** required to complete the task. Also make sure that you have all the necessary materials and tools before you start.

2 **Measure the length** of the awning against the wall; at either end, mark where the 2 expanding bolts are to be inserted.

3 **Drill holes** using an electric drill with a masonry bit. Be sure the holes are the correct depth and diameter for the expanding bolts.

ATTACHING THE AWNING TO THE WALL

1 **Clean out any loose dust** or fragments of masonry from the holes. Insert the expanding bolts (*see inset*) into the holes.

2 **Tighten the bolt** fittings with a wrench. Make sure the expanding parts of the bolts are securely locked into place, and the hooks point up.

3 **Attach one corner** of the canvas awning to the wall by threading an eyelet through one of the wall-mounted hooks. Attach the second corner.

PROVIDING SUPPORT

1 **Once you have attached** both corners of the canvas to the wall, make sure that the awning is taut.

2 **Tie the end** of the nylon cord to the third corner of canvas awning. Repeat for the fourth corner.

3 Attach **each cord** about 3in (8cm) below the top of a post. Leave a little space between the post and awning.

4 **Pound each metal post** deeply and securely into the ground, using the mallet. Be sure that the posts are standing upright.

5 **Knock a tent peg** into the ground about 5ft (1.5m) away from each post using the mallet. Angle the pegs away from the post at about 70°.

6 **Loop each cord** around a tent peg, and use a slip knot to tension the cord. If necessary, use the 2 spare tent pegs to stabilize the posts.

7 **The finished awning** should be securely supported by the metal posts and wall-mounted hooks. It can be removed without difficulty for cleaning, easy storage, or if shade is no longer needed.

CREATING AREAS FOR PLAY

THERE ARE FEW LIMITS to the types of play area that can be built for children, and to reach an appropriate final decision, always begin by considering the age and ability of the children concerned, and plan to scale. Toddlers will be at unnecessary risk if they are allowed to use equipment designed for older children, so add more adventurous apparatus as they grow. Seek the advice of your local authorities for any specific recommendations or guidelines, which you may want to incorporate into the design of your play area.

BUILDING AN ADVENTURE PLAY AREA

Children love active play, and the more ways they have to swing, slide, and jump the better. Naturally, this type of play is not without risk, so the aim should be to create an environment that makes the children think they are being daredevils and taking huge risks, when in actual fact they are in a safe, controlled play area.

Whatever type of adventure play area is constructed, safety must be the over-riding factor. If possible, use wood with smooth or rounded edges, and make sure that the ends of all bolts, screws, and nails do not stick out – they must be recessed into the wood. To prevent toppling, secure all heavy play structures into the soil with deep ground anchors, and if there is a danger of

falling, always soften the play area's surface with a thick covering of wood chips or equivalent. When the structure is complete, examine it thoroughly for potential hazards, and remedy these before you allow children free access; repeat these safety checks regularly.

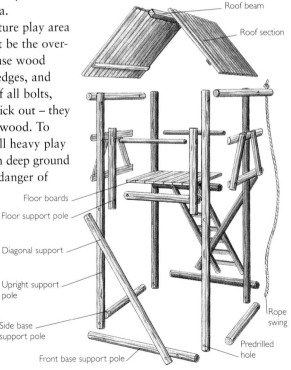

HOW THE TOWER
FITS TOGETHER
Like all kits, this climbing tower comes with detailed instructions. The wood is predrilled, and all fixtures are supplied. A minimum of two adults is needed for assembly, because of the weight of the components.

Roof beam

Roof section

Floor boards

Floor support pole

Diagonal support

Upright support pole

Side base support pole

Front base support pole

Rope swing

Predrilled hole

◀ PROTECTED ADVENTURE *This timber climbing tower and slide is set into a floor of bark chips.*

YOU NEED

- 1 play tower with slide in kit form
- 1½in (4cm) screws
- 6in (15cm) bolts
- 4in (10cm) lag screws
- 2in (5cm) nails
- 20 × 8ft (2.5m) wooden ties
- 6in (15cm) nails
- 9in (22cm) nails
- 4 × 24in (60cm) ground anchors
- 150sq ft (15sq m) geotextile fabric
- Roofing nails
- 150cu ft (5cu m) wood chips
- Hammer
- Small wood block
- Screwdriver
- Socket wrench
- Wrench
- Tape measure
- Pencil and string
- Marker pegs
- Electric drill
- Builder's set square
- Hand saw
- Medium sandpaper
- Spade
- Knife or scissors

ASSEMBLING THE PLAY TOWER FRAME

1 **Line up** the front upright support poles on the ground. Here, 2 short support poles are placed inside 2 long support poles. Align the predrilled holes (*see inset*) and drive the front rung through them to join the support poles together.

2 **Lift the front section** on its side and ask a helper to support the upper pole while the front rung is fitted firmly into place. Always place a small wood block between the hammer and poles to prevent damage. Attach the rung with 2 1½in (4cm) screws.

3 **Lower the front section** back to the ground, and align a floor support pole on the inside. Hammer 2 bolts through predrilled holes (*see inset*); tighten the nuts with a socket wrench.

4 **Turn the frame over** and fit the front base support pole to the bottom of the 2 long support poles. Use 2 bolts in the predrilled holes, and tighten them with the same wrench.

5 **Turn over the frame.** Position a diagonal support at the front, across the lower half of the long support poles. Secure with 2 lag screws and tighten with a wrench (*see inset*). The diagonal support will strengthen the front section. Build the back section in the same way as the front.

ATTACHING THE SIDE SECTIONS OF THE TOWER

1 **Lay the front** and back sections on their sides, and ask a helper to hold them in position. Join the sections together at the top by bolting on the left roof support pole. This support pole is longer than the right roof support because it will eventually anchor the rope swing into the tower.

2 **Position a side** base support pole. This should be in alignment with the front and back base support poles.

3 **Fit the base** support pole using 2 lag screws. Make sure all of the joints are fully tightened and secure.

4 **Fit side rails** to the upper half of the side section. Turn over the tower and complete the other side in the same way.

MAKING THE ROOF

1 **Fit the roof beam** to one of the prefabricated roof sections using 4 lag screws in the predrilled holes.

2 **Tip both roof sections** onto their ends and join the second section securely to the roof beam.

3 **The finished roof** should be strong enough to stand freely. It is now ready to be attached to the tower.

FINISHING THE PLAY TOWER

1 **Move the roof** into place at the top of the tower. Fasten it to the roof support poles with 8 lag screws.

2 **Double check** all the joints to make sure that all lag screws and other nuts and bolts are fully tightened to protect the joints from excessive movement and wear. Rotate the tower to check the remaining joints.

3 **Lift the tower** into its standing position. The structure will be heavy, so enlist the help of at least one other adult. Do not allow children to go near the tower until it is firmly anchored into the ground (*see p.60*).

4 **Nail the floorboards** onto the back and front floor support poles. Use 4 nails to secure each floorboard.

ASSEMBLING THE PLAY TOWER LADDER

1 **Lay out** the ladder sections to make sure you have all the parts and that all the holes have been predrilled.

2 **Evenly measure and mark** out positions for the rungs on the ladder poles at 14in (35cm) intervals.

3 **Fit the rungs** into position using a wrench and 2 lag screws per rung. Make sure no screws protrude.

4 **Position the ladder** beneath the back floor support pole at the rear of the tower. One side of the ladder will rest on the back diagonal support.

5 **Fasten the ladder** securely to the underside of the back floor support pole using 2 lag screws. The ladder should be strong enough to hold an adult's weight.

ATTACHING THE ROPE SWING TO THE TOWER

1 **Climb onto the tower** using the ladder; ask a helper to steady the tower. Thread the rope swing through the predrilled hole in the left roof support pole.

2 **Tie a knot** in the top end of the rope swing to prevent it from pulling back through the hole in the left roof support pole. Make sure the knot is tight and very secure.

CONSTRUCTING THE PLAY AREA SURFACE

MARKING OUT

• Allow enough space on all sides of play equipment to keep children from running into dangerous objects.

• Rather than use a builder's square, which may be too small for large areas, measure right angles with marker pegs, a tape measure, and string. Any triangle with sides measured to the ratio of 3:4:5 – i.e., 4ft (1.2m) × 5ft (1.6m) × 6½ft (2m) – will include a right angle.

1 Measure and mark out the play area using a tape measure, string, and marker pegs. Check that all corners are at right angles by measuring a 3:4:5 triangle at each one (*see box, left*). Be sure the surface is level, so any play structures will be stable.

2 Lay out the wooden ties along the boundary of the marked-out play area. With an electric drill, make pilot holes for the nails where the joints are to be made.

3 Fasten the joints together using 6in (15cm) nails hammered through the pilot holes and into the ties. Make sure the nail heads do not protrude from the pilot holes.

4 Measure and mark the last ties that have to be cut to size. For accurate, right-angled joints, always use a builder's set square.

5 Cut each tie along the marked line carefully with a hand saw to keep all edges square. Smooth down rough edges with sandpaper.

6 Position a second layer of ties on top of the first so all joints overlap. Join the top to the bottom ties with 9in (22cm) nails.

PUTTING IN GROUND ANCHORS

1 **Mark the ground** to show the desired position of the base of the play tower. Dig a hole about 15in (38cm) deep at each corner. Leave the dug-out soil next to the holes.

2 **Twist a ground anchor** into the bottom of each hole using a wrench. Keep twisting until the tip of the ground anchor is firmly embedded in the soil.

3 **Fill in each hole** around its ground anchor with the loose dirt. Firm the soil frequently as the hole is filled to make sure that the anchor is well secured.

4 **Once buried,** the hooked ends of the anchors should be protruding at equal heights from the ground so they can be attached to the legs of the play tower.

5 **Secure ground anchors** are now in position inside the walled play area. Make sure the retaining wall is strong and stable, because it will have to withstand a lot of wear. The play area is now ready to be lined and filled with wood chips (*see pp.60–61*).

LINING THE PLAY AREA

1 **Spread out** the geotextile fabric so that it covers the entire area inside the retaining walls of the play area. It may be necessary to tack the fabric to the wooden planks to prevent it from blowing around while it is being laid. Make sure any joins or seams in the fabric overlap by at least 12in (30cm).

2 **Cut a small slit** above each of the ground anchors to allow them to penetrate the fabric. Try to make the slit as small as possible.

3 **Push the fabric down** so that it lies flat against the ground and the ground anchors protrude through. Smooth out any wrinkles.

4 **Fasten the fabric** to the inside of the retaining wall using roofing nails. Space the nails about 12–15in (30–38cm) apart.

POSITIONING THE PLAY TOWER

1 **Move the play tower** into place so that each of the 4 upright support poles are positioned next to a ground anchor. The assembled tower is heavy and awkward to move, and the geotextile fabric can be quite slippery to work on, so this job must be done by at least 2 adults.

2 **Bolt the tower** firmly to ground anchors using 4 carriage bolts and a socket wrench. Afterward, make sure that the tower is level and completely stable.

FINISHING OFF THE ADVENTURE PLAY AREA

WOOD CHIPS

• A layer of wood chips 6in (15cm) deep is often enough to break a child's fall. Check with your local authorities to find out if there are any guidelines or regulations.

• Wood chips are best laid over a geotextile fabric, which excludes weeds while allowing water to drain away.

• Wood chips are expensive if bought by the bag. A local lumber yard may be able to supply a bulk load for a reasonable price.

1 **Maneuver the plastic slide** to meet the floorboards of the tower. Make sure both ends of the slide are level so it will not twist when in use.

2 **Attach the top** of the slide to the tower floor with 2 4cm (1½in) screws. Make sure the heads of the screws do not stick out.

3 **Spread wood chips** over the entire play area. A depth of at least 6in (15cm) should be laid for it to be effective (*see box, right*). The wood chip surface will need to be raked regularly to make sure that airborne weeds do not become established and that the heavily used areas retain a full depth of chips. Occasionally, the entire surface may need to be filled up.

4 **The finished adventure play area** is now ready for use, and it should last for many years. As a precautionary measure, however, check the stability of the structure and the tightness of all bolts and screws at least once a year, preferably in dry weather. Also, smooth any roughened parts of the wood. Cracks will develop along the grain of rounded wood; this is not a defect but part of the natural aging process.

MAKING A SANDBOX

This 15sq ft (1.2sq m) sandbox is quite simple to construct, and it occupies a very small area of yard space. It is built of industrial-grade plywood, which is light, strong, and weather-resistant, and it has a cover to keep the sand contained and dry, and free from fouling by birds and pets. Once filled, this sandbox will accommodate three young children comfortably.

PREPARING THE SITE

YOU NEED
• 4 paving slabs 24 × 24in (60 × 60cm)
• 50sq ft (5sq m) industrial plywood
• 8 metal brackets
• ½in (1.5cm) screws
• Child-safe wood preservative or paint
• 1100lb (500kg) play sand
• 24in (60cm) rope
• Tape measure
• 4 bamboo stakes
• String and pencil
• Spade and rake
• Level
• Mallet
• Set square and saw
• Screwdriver
• Medium sandpaper
• Paintbrush
• Electric drill

1 **Measure and mark** a square 4 × 4ft (1.2 × 1.2m). The diagonal measurements will match each other if the area is square.

2 **Tie string** around the base of the bamboo stakes to mark out the square. The string will act as a guide for digging the hole.

3 **Dig a hole** 16in (40cm) deep, inside the string line. Make sure that the sides are smooth and vertical (*see inset*). Place the loose soil just outside the hole .

PUTTING IN THE BASE

1 **Compact the soil** in the base of the hole. If it is difficult to level the soil, cover it with a bed of sand 2in (5cm) deep.

2 **Lay the paving slabs** at the bottom of the pit, and with a level, make sure that each one is level as you lay it. If necessary, gently tap the slabs with the handle of a mallet until they are level. Continue until all 4 slabs are laid in a square.

MAKING THE WALLS

1 **Measure out a section** of heavy-duty industrial plywood for one side panel of the sandbox. The section should be 24in (60cm) wide by 4ft (1.2m) long. Use a builder's set square to make sure all the corners are accurate right angles. Cut the first section using a hand saw.

2 **In each corner,** about 1½in (4cm) in from the edge, mark the position to which the brackets will be attached.

3 **Measure and mark out** the remaining 3 strips of wood to the same dimensions as before (*see step 1*).

4 **Saw carefully** along the saw lines to make 3 more side panels. As before, mark the position of the corner brackets.

ASSEMBLING THE FRAME

1 **For each panel,** place one bracket on its mark in the top right corner of the panel and mark the screw holes. Fasten each bracket with 2 screws to form a corner joint.

2 **Join the 4 panels** together to form a box by attaching the first 4 corner brackets at the top of the panels. Turn the box over and screw in the bottom 4 corner brackets.

FINISHING THE SANDBOX

1 **Insert the box** into the hole so that it sits just on the edge of the paved floor. If you have laid the paving and made the box correctly, the top of the box should be level.

2 **Smooth off** any splinters or sharp edges on the box with sandpaper to make it safe for children to use. An electric drill with a sanding attachment will make this job easier.

3 **Treat the outer** surfaces of the sandbox with a wood preservative. When the paint is dry, bank up the dirt around the sides.

4 **Fill the sandbox** with washed or play sand to within 6in (15cm) of the top. Spread the sand with a rake as it goes in, which will make it simpler to fill the sandbox evenly.

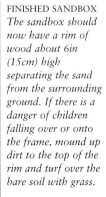

FINISHED SANDBOX
The sandbox should now have a rim of wood about 6in (15cm) high separating the sand from the surrounding ground. If there is a danger of children falling over or onto the frame, mound up dirt to the top of the rim and turf over the bare soil with grass.

MAKING A LID FOR THE SANDBOX

1 Measure the dimensions of the sandbox (that is, the width and length) to calculate the area needed to be covered by the lid – about 15sq ft (1.2sq m). Mark out a section of industrial plywood a bit larger than these measurements so the lid will have a lip.

SANDBOX TIPS

• Young children must be supervised at all times, so place the sandbox in plain view of the house.
• Never use builder's sand for a sandbox. Play sand is cleaner and softer.
• When building a sandbox, buy more sand than needed; it will need to be filled up from time to time.

2 Cut the plywood to size with a hand saw, then smooth down all sharp or rough edges on the lid with sandpaper to remove the danger of splinters.

3 Treat the lid with the same wood preservative that was used for the sandbox. Support the lid above the ground so that it is easier to reach and paint. Allow it to dry.

4 Drill 2 holes 6in (15cm) apart, centered along one edge. Pass a 12in (30cm) length of rope through the holes; knot the ends to form a handle.

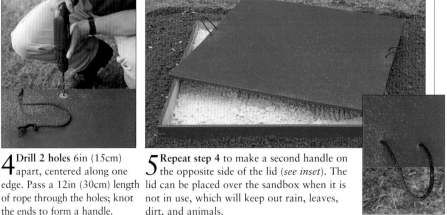

5 Repeat step **4** to make a second handle on the opposite side of the lid (*see inset*). The lid can be placed over the sandbox when it is not in use, which will keep out rain, leaves, dirt, and animals.

GETTING DOWN TO BASICS

PRACTICAL MATTERS

FOR ANY CONSTRUCTION TASK to progress smoothly and to achieve the desired result, it is important to have the right tools and equipment for the job in hand. Just "making do" is never enough and involves compromises that may well lead to inferior workmanship. Gather all tools and equipment beforehand to make sure everything is available; a job can take twice as long as necessary if every accessory has to be searched for and found before it can be used.

TOOLS FOR THE JOB

Quality tools are essential for construction work, even though the initial cost may be high; they should be seen as a long-term investment. Specialized tools for infrequent use can be rented (*see box, right*). To keep tools in top condition, be sure that they are cleaned and stored in a dry place after use.

Construction tools fall into three categories: woodworking tools, such as saws and chisels; building tools, like shovels and masonry drills; and general-purpose tools, such as levels and hammers.

RENTAL TOOLS

• Some of the most useful specialized tools for garden construction are cement mixers, stone or block cutters, and chain saws; they are available from most tool-rental stores.

• Protective clothing and safety equipment can be rented at the same time as the tools.

• Always get a demonstration of how any machinery works before you take it away.

• A good rental store will offer advice and usually rent tools by the full or half-day.

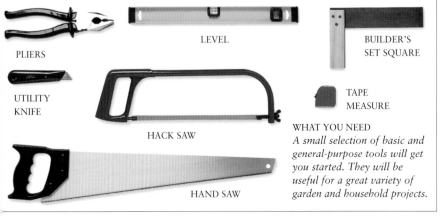

PLIERS

LEVEL

BUILDER'S SET SQUARE

UTILITY KNIFE

TAPE MEASURE

HACK SAW

HAND SAW

WHAT YOU NEED
A small selection of basic and general-purpose tools will get you started. They will be useful for a great variety of garden and household projects.

DEFINED AREAS *Different equipment is needed to manage different areas of the garden.*

USING RAW MATERIALS

D ECIDING ON WHICH MATERIALS TO USE depends on a number of factors. For example, how long is the structure is expected to last? Ultimately, this boils down to quality and subsequent cost, but it is always good practice to select the best and most appropriate materials you can afford. Safety is also an important factor, especially around children and the elderly. For instance, wooden materials should be solidly built and smooth to reduce the risk of injury during use.

HARD MATERIALS

These are the materials used for long-lasting structures, such as brick barbecues and patios. It is worth taking the time to seek expert advice before making a final choice. Consider the following questions: will the material be damaged by winter weather? Will it be too hot to touch on an average summer's day? Will it crack as it ages? If available, reclaimed or recycled materials can make a new feature look established more quickly, but they can be much more expensive than using new ones.

BUILDING BRICKS
A wide range is available, but their durability varies considerably. Most types are man-made, although some bricks are natural stone.

BRICKS FOR GROUNDWORK
Bricks can be laid in the ground instead of paving slabs, but make sure that the bricks are frostproof and nonslip.

PAVING SLABS
Much solid groundwork is prepared with paving slabs. Choose between natural stone or cast concrete in a range of colors and textures.

KEY CONSIDERATIONS

• Heavy garden structures made from hard materials need proper foundations. An unstable structure is dangerous, so seek professional advice and always leave the ambitious jobs to a professional.
• Moving hard materials – even single paving slabs – is heavy work, so try to recruit a team of helpers.
• Choose hard materials that match and complement the design, color, and age of your house and garden.
• Make sure that hard materials for outdoor use are completely weather resistant.

LOOSE MATERIALS

Landscaping and surfacing materials, such as gravel, pebbles, wood chips, and play sand are described as loose materials, and they are often supplied in bags. Wood chips are popular for children's play areas since they provide a soft landing pad, and they are also used as a garden mulch. Washed sand is used for sandboxes, while gravel is favored for some play areas as well as being a popular alternative to a lawn.

It can be a false economy to choose loose materials simply on the basis of cost. If at all possible, inspect a sample before ordering, especially if you have little experience of the materials available. Then, select only those materials that come from a reputable source. Potentially harmful impurities include sharp stones, weeds, splintered wood or metal, or chemical residues that may stain or burn the skin.

WASHED SAND   SLATE CHIPS   GRAVEL   PEBBLES   WOOD CHIPS

WOODEN MATERIALS

The range of lumber available for outdoor use can be intimidating if you are not familiar with the different types. Most is seasoned or kiln-dried softwood, normally treated with a preservative to extend its useful life to approximately 20–25 years.

Hardwood, such as beech or oak, is less common mainly because it is far more expensive, but it has a greater resistance to rot, lasting up to 30–40 years.

Reconstituted wood, like industrial-grade plywood, is made up of several layers of thin wood sheeting bonded together with glue. This material offers high strength and durability at a relatively low price.

SELECTION OF WOOD
The three main types of lumber for outdoor use are softwood, hardwood, and industrial-grade plywood. Try to use products that have been treated with a wood preservative.

INDUSTRIAL-GRADE PLYWOOD

PRESSURE-TREATED SOFTWOOD

HARDWOOD

UNTREATED SOFTWOOD

GROUND SHEETING MATERIALS

Many garden construction projects involve the use of ground sheeting, either to retain loose materials, to suppress weeds, or to keep a water feature watertight. The type chosen will be dictated by the situation.

Impermeable membranes are ideal for ponds and other water features, as they are durable and waterproof. Vinyl, PVC, and plastic are common examples, available in a range of thicknesses.

Permeable membranes are used to line areas of wood chips, play sand, or gravel. Not only do they stop soil and weeds mixing with the loose materials they also allow water to drain away freely. The spun or woven covering membranes are the most flexible, yet they are still very hard-wearing and difficult to rip or tear. Many are designed to last more than 25 years.

◄ PVC LINER
The thickest grades of PVC last the longest. More flexible than plastic.

◄ GEOTEXTILE FABRIC
Permeable liner that suppresses weeds but allows rainwater to pass.

◄ VINYL LINER
The best watertight membrane; it is very flexible, hard-wearing, and easy to repair (see p.75).

MORTAR AND CONCRETE

At its simplest, mortar or concrete is made by mixing sand and cement together, then adding some water. Like cooking, however, different recipes suit different purposes and occasions, and it is critical to use the right one or the project may lack stability and strength (*see box, below*). Masonry mortar is used for brickwork, dry mortar is used for pointing gaps in old walls or paving stones, and bedding mortar is used for laying and jointing paving. Concrete is basically mortar with added aggregate (crushed stone or gravel) and is ideal for wall footings and foundations.

Four parts sand

One part cement

Sand and cement mix

MORTAR MIX
Four parts sand to one part cement makes building mortar. Use an equal mixture of sharp sand (for pliability) and soft sand (to bind the mix).

MIXING RECIPES

All parts for these recipes are by volume:
Masonry mortar for building walls: 4 parts soft/sharp sand mixed; 1 part cement.
Dry mortar: same recipe as above, but with less water added to make a stiffer mix.
Bedding mortar: 5 parts sharp sand; 1 part cement.
Concrete: 2 parts coarse aggregate; 2 parts soft sand; 1 part cement.
Pouring concrete: 2½ parts coarse aggregate; 1½ parts sharp sand; 1 part cement.

A chemical additive can be added to mortar, which will increase the pliability of the mixture and extend its longevity. This makes mortar easier to use, especially if you are working slowly.

ORDERING, DELIVERY, AND STORAGE

When ordering materials, establish whether the price includes a delivery charge or tax, and whether a bulk discount is available. Find out the size of the delivery vehicle, as this may determine how close to your property the order can be delivered, and ask if the materials arrive loose, which takes up far more room, or in bags. For any deliveries that are to be unloaded onto a public road, it is advisable to notify the local highway department, especially if the goods are to remain there overnight.

Building materials often take up a lot of space, so consider where they are to be stored safely until you use them. Powdered materials like cement, which can absorb water and harden, must be kept in a dry place in sealed, waterproof bags. Bricks and lumber must be stored on boards or pallets to keep them off the ground and covered with plastic film to protect them from the weather. Ideally, wood should be stored level and flat to prevent it from buckling and twisting out of shape.

ESTIMATING QUANTITIES

Most suppliers are very helpful when it comes to estimating quantities of materials required for outdoor projects, although they do need a little help. On a sheet of graph paper, mark out the dimensions involved to calculate the area or volume. A supplier can work from these calculations and estimate the quantities of materials required (*see below*).

Material	Approximate coverage
36 bricks (laid flat)	10sq ft (1sq m)
54 bricks (laid on edge)	10sq ft (1sq m)
45 pavers	10sq ft (1sq m)
4 paving slabs 24×24in (60×60cm)	15sq ft (1.5sq m)
220lb (100kg) cobble-stones 2×3in (5×8cm)	11sq in (70sq cm)
220lb (100kg) loose gravel 1in (2.5cm) deep	30sq ft (3sq m)
220lb (100kg) rolled gravel 2in (5cm) deep	12½sq ft (1.2sq m)
220lb (100kg) bedding sand 2in (5cm) deep	25sq ft (2.5sq m)
220lb (100kg) sharp sand 2in (5cm) deep	20sq ft (2sq m)

A GLOSSARY OF USEFUL TERMS

Aggregate
Crushed stone or gravel used as an ingredient in concrete; ¾in (20mm) aggregate is suitable for most concreting jobs.

Cement
A gray powder that contains limestone. Mixed with water and sand, it forms the bonding agent in mortar and concrete.

Concrete
A mixture of sand, cement, and aggregate. It forms a hardened material, which can be used in construction or for surfacing.

Foundation
A solid base made from concrete for a wall, building, or other heavy structure.

Geotextile fabric
A woven or spun lining material that allows water to pass through it, while simultaneously preventing the penetration of weeds.

Gravel
A mix of small pebbles, pea gravel, and crushed stone such as compactible gravel, which is made up of larger stone pieces combined with smaller particles. Available in various grades; used for paths, ½in (12mm) is about maximum for walking comfort.

Mortar
A mixture of sand, cement powder, and water. It is used in construction to bond bricks, stones, or slabs.

Sand
Soft, or builders', sand is fine-grade; used in mortar, it makes a more binding mix. Sharp sand is coarser and gives mortar a more pliable texture. Washed sand is safe for children's sandboxes.

Shuttering
A temporary wooden framework to hold wet concrete in place while it sets.

Wood
Softwood, such as pine, is often cheaper and less resistant to rot than hardwood, such as ash or walnut, which is sometimes harder to cut. Plywood consists of several thin layers of wood glued together; it is strong and relatively inexpensive.

MAINTENANCE, SAFETY, AND REPAIR

Safety must be a constant priority for any garden construction, from the original plan and building work, right through the project's completion and beyond, making sure that it remains safe and sturdy for as long as possible. Regular maintenance helps, such as an annual coating of wood preservative or the oiling of moving metal parts (chains, bolts, and hinges, for example), and remember to repair or replace worn or damaged components as they appear.

PROTECTIVE CLOTHING AND EQUIPMENT

A major proportion of household accidents occur when working in the yard, but many hazards can be greatly reduced. Lift heavy items safely by using the correct posture, or get someone to help with really heavy objects. Never wear loose or flapping clothing, which may catch on moving machinery. Use sturdy gloves to protect hands when working with rough materials, such as bricks or sawed wood. Kneeling mats and knee pads are useful if a lot of kneeling is required, and it is advisable to wear a hard hat when working on a structure taller than 6ft (2m).

POWER TOOL SAFETY

- Wear eye protection at all times.
- If the equipment creates large amounts of dust, wear a face mask.
- For noisy tools, such as stone cutters or chain saws, wear ear protection.
- Use circuit breakers with all electrical tools.
- Do not use an electrical tool during or just after rain, as this may cause electric shocks.
- Always disconnect electrical tools before adjusting, cleaning, or inspecting. Never touch a damaged wire without disconnecting it.

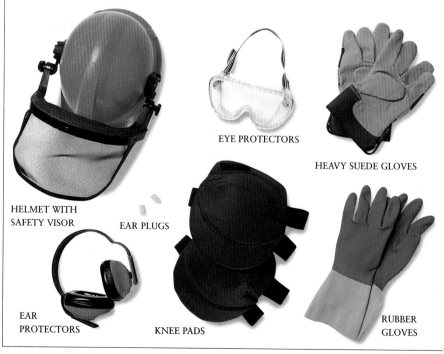

EYE PROTECTORS

HEAVY SUEDE GLOVES

HELMET WITH
SAFETY VISOR

EAR PLUGS

EAR
PROTECTORS

KNEE PADS

RUBBER
GLOVES

SURFACES AND WALLS

Some surfaces naturally become smooth and even slippery as they age. On steps or ladders, the safest course of action is to replace them once they begin to look worn.

For surfaces that are walked on, a regular scrub and wash with a stiff brush and power hose will remove slippery dirt, moss, and algae. During planning, choose materials with safety in mind. Rather than smooth surfaces, use grooved decking or coarsely surfaced paving slabs to provide the necessary traction in wet conditions, particularly under overhanging trees.

Wooden surfaces, such as fence panels, often have rough surfaces; remove any potentially dangerous splinters with sandpaper. Coat wood every two or three years with a preservative to protect against rot.

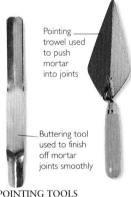

Pointing trowel used to push mortar into joints

Buttering tool used to finish off mortar joints smoothly

POINTING TOOLS
This buttering tool and pointing trowel are needed to repair joints in brickwork and patios. Use them to apply fresh mortar (see p.70).

POINTING A PATIO
Chip out crumbled mortar and brush away dust. Soak the area with water, then work fresh mortar into the gaps. Remove excess mortar as necessary.

WEEDY PAVING
Weeds can be a problem in the cracks of paths or paving. Remove them with weed-killer or by scrubbing with a stiff brush and patio cleaner.

LAWN CARE
Lawns are important outdoor living areas, so they must be cared for properly. Mow regularly and remove moss, weeds, and dead grass.

NONSLIP DECKING
Wooden surfaces can be hazardous when wet. If the wood is not grooved, add a cover of wire mesh, which soon weathers and blends in.

LOOSE SURFACES

- Gravel, sand, and wood chips can be difficult to keep clean. Soil is one contaminant, and it carries weed seeds, which must be removed as they germinate.
- Broken glass is a dangerous contaminant. To be certain, replace all the loose material in an affected area.
- Unfortunately, pets think sandboxes make very inviting toilets. The only effective deterrent is to place a cover over the sandbox when it is not in use.

ELECTRICITY AND WATER

THE USE OF ELECTRICAL EQUIPMENT can save a tremendous amount of time, and it can also take away much of the hard and laborious work of construction. Saws, drills, stone cutters, hammer drills, concrete chisels, and a whole range of other tools are now standard equipment available for home use. Take particular care wherever water and electricity are in close proximity to one another, such as in water features. If possible, always seek expert advice.

ELECTRICAL APPLIANCES

It is always advisable to buy good-quality power tools, many of which are battery powered and incredibly versatile. Other electrical equipment includes items such as garden lighting, and pumps and fountains for water features, which may be run directly from the power supply or through a device that reduces voltage (*see box, below*). Solar-powered equipment is also available, with a negligible risk of electric shock, although the technology does have its obvious limitations.

CIRCUIT BREAKER (GFCI)
Always use a ground fault circuit interrupter , which cuts off the electricity if there is a short. This adapter fits between the plug and socket.

TIMER
It is easy to forget to switch outdoor lights on or off. This programmable timer, which fits into a socket, allows for automatic control.

EXTENSION CABLE
Outdoors, use a heavy duty, grounded extension cable with watertight connections. A coiled cable is less likely interfere with machinery.

PROTECTED CABLE
All electric wiring outdoors must be armored or protected by an easily seen conduit, for example, this brightly colored hose.

HIGH AND LOW VOLTAGE

• For high voltage electricity outdoors, all wiring, connections, and fixture must be installed by a qualified electrician. The system must also be protected by a ground fault circuit interrupter (GFCI or circuit breaker).

• Low voltage systems are used in conjunction with a transformer, which should be sited indoors, close to the wall socket. A transformer converts high voltage to low voltage, which presents no danger from electric shock.

• Low voltage appliances have a limited output and are suitable only for small water features or decorative lighting.

• High voltage systems are essential for bright lights and large watercourses, but don't forget the circuit breaker.

OUTDOOR WATER FEATURES

A water feature looks good only when it runs well, which means that the pump must be maintained and cleaned at least once every year (see below), and the water may need to be cleaned, filled up, or replaced. Any structures that are part of the design should also be checked; an unsteady rock or brick, for example, is a potential hazard.

Special care must also be taken during extreme weather. Fill up the water levels regularly during hot, dry periods. In freezing weather ice expands, which will put great pressure on the liner or water tank. If possible, drain and disconnect the water feature until warmer weather; otherwise, use a pond heater and insulate sensitive plants with canvas sheeting.

WATER SAFETY

• Even shallow water can be dangerous, particularly for small children, who find water irresistible. A barrier, such as a low wire fence or a grill on top of the water (see below), can be effective, although it may look unsightly.
• A submersible pump must have enough cable to extend onto dry land. This avoids having to connect cables underwater. All other cables should be kept above water level.

METAL GRILL IMPROVES WATER SAFETY

MENDING A LEAK

A hole in a flexible liner is relatively easy to repair, like a puncture on a bicycle tire. Most repair kits require warm, dry conditions to get good contact between the liner and the repair patch, although some adhesives work underwater (see far right).

For adhesive tape or repair patches, the liner must first be allowed to dry, then brush the damaged surface clean and wipe with mineral spirits. Cut a patch at least twice the size of the damaged area, and if necessary, cover both surfaces with bonding adhesive. Press the patch down firmly to ensure good contact. Leave for 24 hours, then refill the water feature.

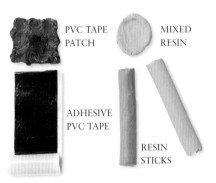

PVC TAPE PATCH

MIXED RESIN

ADHESIVE PVC TAPE

RESIN STICKS

LINER REPAIR KITS
Adhesive PVC tape must be applied to a dry pond liner. The resin is an adaptable sealant that can be used underwater.

HOW TO TAKE APART AND CLEAN A WATER PUMP

Most pumps are fitted with a filter to catch any dirt or debris before it enters the motor, so this filter must be cleaned at least once a year or as recommended by the manufacturer. Switch off the power, and remove the pump from the water. The outer casing usually opens up to allow removal of the filter and inspection of the delivery pipes and propeller. The motor itself is usually a sealed unit that cannot be opened without causing irreversible damage.

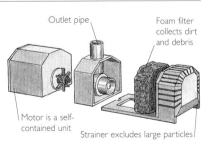

Outlet pipe

Foam filter collects dirt and debris

Motor is a self-contained unit

Strainer excludes large particles

EATING AND ENTERTAINING AREAS

A YARD USED FOR ENTERTAINING usually needs lots of furniture, a bit of food and drink, and as the sun begins to set, some heat and light may be called for too. To prepare, be sure that all food-preparation surfaces are clean and hygienic, check that outdoor furniture is safe and well maintained, and position barbecues, lamps, and candles completely out of harm's way, especially if children are present. With all this taken care of, sit back and enjoy yourself.

MAINTAINING OUTDOOR FURNITURE

All outdoor furniture should be wiped down with a sponge and soapy water at least once a year and any upholstery allowed to dry. Wooden furniture will benefit from an annual coating of wood preservative, and metal or plastic-coated metal should be checked for signs of rust (*see below*). Always lubricate moving joints well, and in cold climates, store or cover furniture to keep it out of the worst of the weather.

FROST-DAMAGED UMBRELLA BASE
Winter storage is a priority in cold climates. This water-filled umbrella base should have been drained and stored; instead it froze and ruptured.

COLORED WOOD PRESERVATIVES
Wood preservatives can be combined with wood stains to rejuvenate and protect old or faded wooden furniture.

DEALING WITH RUST

Inspect metals structures regularly for any signs of rust or corrosion caused by damage or gradual wear. Remove any loose rust with sandpaper and apply a rustproof paint. Always examine plastic-coated metal furniture, play equipment, or tools carefully; any cracks will expose the metal to corrosion, which may be hidden under the plastic.

RUSTY LADDER
Welded joints and hollow ends of tubes are vulnerable to rust. Sand down the affected area, then treat it with a rustproof paint.

RUST REPAIR

• The best and cheapest way to minimize rust is to wash and dry metal furniture weekly and to store it in a dry place when not in use.

• Badly corroded joints and fixtures should never be ignored because they can snag fingers or skin, causing injuries.

• Major rust damage can compromise the safety of a metal structure, especially if it has to bear the weight of a child or adult. If you have any doubt, get a replacement.

BARBECUE SAFETY AND EQUIPMENT

Barbecues and grills reach very high temperatures and will quickly cause severe burns when their hot surfaces come into contact with skin; for this reason, you should wear an apron and oven gloves, and use the correct utensils (*see below*). Keep children out of reach of any open flames, heaters, and barbecues, not just when they are in operation but for a safe period afterward until they have cooled. Hot water from a pan can still injure a child up to 30 minutes after it has boiled.

FIRE SAFETY

• Always have at least one general-purpose fire extinguisher and a fire blanket close at hand where open flames are being used.
• Store all flammable materials in a cool, dark, fireproof place away from the house.
• Where bottles of compressed gas are used as a fuel source, always check any rubberized connections for signs of deterioration or potential leaks, especially after storage.
• Never use a flame to test for drafts or fuel leaks.

CHARCOAL   WATER SPRAY   GLOVES

NEWSPAPERS

FIRELIGHTERS

SAFETY MATCHES

APRON   COOKING UTENSILS

BARBECUE EQUIPMENT
Outdoor cooking requires special equipment. Protective gear for a barbecue chef includes long-handled tools, gloves, and an apron.

LAMPS AND CANDLES

Open flames should always be treated with caution and viewed as a potential hazard. As a rule, it is never wise to carry lamps, lanterns, or candles while they are lit or still hot, and they must be kept well away from flammable fabric, such as umbrellas and awnings, and activity areas – where they may be knocked over. Enclose candles in glass tubes, old jars, or in lanterns. With oil lamps and lanterns, store them empty or with just enough oil present to prevent the wick from drying out. If they become damaged and cannot be repaired by an expert, they must be discarded.

ENCLOSED   CANDLE IN   OIL LAMP
LANTERN   GLASS TUBE

INDEX

Page numbers in **bold italics** indicate illustrations.

ACKNOWLEDGMENTS

Picture Research Anna Grapes
Picture Librarian Romaine Werblow

Special photography Peter Anderson,
Trish Gant, Gary Ombler

Illustrations Karen Gavin

Index Hilary Bird

Dorling Kindersley would like to thank: all
staff at the RHS, in particular Susanne Mitchell,
Karen Wilson, and Barbara Haynes at Vincent
Square, and Dean Peckett at Wisley; Joanna
Chisholm for editorial assistance and Ann
Thompson for design assistance; Gillian
Fountain and Chris Clunn at **Loddon Valley
Garden Toys** (www.lvgt.co.uk) for supply and
construction of the adventure play-ground;
Andy Christou at **Maya Solar**
(www.mayasolar.co.uk) for the loan of solar-
powered equipment; Roy Card and David
Dodd at **The Outdoor Room Ltd** (tel: 01372
742293) for construction of the barbecue; and
Martin Crow at **Southern Pergola**
(www.southern-pergola.demon.co.uk) for
supply and construction of the gazebo.

American Horticultural Society
Visit the AHS at www.ahs.org or call them
at 1-800-777-7631 ext. 119. Membership
benefits include *The American Gardener*
magazine, free admission to flower shows, the
free seed exchange, book services, and the
Gardener's Information Service.

Photography
The publisher would also like to thank the
following for their kind permission to
reproduce their photographs:
(key: t=top, c=center, b=below, l=left, r=right)

From the B&Q 2000 range: 6, 8b, 10bl, 11t,
12cl, 12br, 13tl, 13cr, 15br, 23bl.
Garden Picture Library: A. I. Lord 23br; J. S.
Sira 15t; Ron Sutherland 19tl.
John Glover: 2, 9tl, 14b, 24br, 30.
Jerry Harpur: Brian Berry 28br; Sonny Garcia
9br; Victor Nelson 21cr.
Indian Ocean Trading Company
(www.indian-ocean.co.uk): 17bl, 19br.
Photos Horticultural: 4bl, 24cl, 25t.
Ring Lighting Outdoor Range: 20bl, 20br,
22cl, 22t.
Steven Wooster: jacket back tr.